Written in the Body

Written in the Body

Elisa A. Garza

Mouthfeel Press is an indie press. We publish works in
English and Spanish by new and established poets and
writers. We publish poetry, fiction, and non-fiction.

Cover Design: Enzo Rodríquez Suárez
Interior Design: Kimberly James

Contact Information:
Mouthfeelbooks.com
Info.mouthfeelbooks@gmail.com

ISBN: 978-1-957840-44-4

Published in the United States, 2025

First Printing in English
$15

MOUTHFEEL PRESS

Protocol

I. Diagnosed and Treated

The Body Betrays   1

Casual Conversation   2

Abecedary of Chemotherapy   3

Presurgical Scan   4

Radiant Hope   5

Radiation Bestiary   6

Directions   7

Found: Letters and Advertisements

    One Year After Diagnosis   8

To My Chest Muscles, for Defending Against an

    Implantable Port, One Year Later 11

II. Locally Recurrent

Hues the Rainbow Reveals   15

Animal Vegetable Mineral   17

Postsurgical Confessions   18

I Am the Shores   19

Stitches   20

In Between Treatments   21

Relationship Status: Complicated   22

The Femme Explains Her Deconstruction   23

Self and Other Findings   24

III. Metastasized

If you think about it,   27

Poem Serum   29

Boring and Routine   30

Seeking   32

Challenging the Colonizer   34

Microcosm   36

Easy   38

The Least   39

Without End   41

Notes and Acknowledgments

About the Author

For the family I have lost to cancer:

Helen, Marta, Dora, Guillermo, Raquel, Javier, Delma, and Eduardo

I

Diagnosed and Treated

The Body Betrays

One cell starts humming off key,
just enough, then others join,
soon a chorus of vibrations,

a fresh voice, and the body listens.

Oh so subtly, the new choir,
their debut song, persuades, persuades.

Singing softly, they settle and they grow
in number, in harmony. They belong.

Emboldened, cells roam, move beyond
the cluster in their concert hall,
teaching others new sounds,

colonizing, spreading song into lymph,
creating a vascular tune
unchallenged. This, you see, is how.

Casual Conversation

for Erika Solberg

"How did they find your cancer,"
the radiology technician asked me
while I removed my bra behind the curtain
before he x-rayed my lungs.
"I found my cancer," I said.
My hope that it would resolve on its own,
a rogue lactation mastitis,
milk dropping a dozen years late,
I didn't say, because he wouldn't have understood.
A few weeks ago, I needed to believe that
the lump was nothing to worry about
because denial is the first stage of grief.

Because denial is the first stage of grief,
the lump was nothing to worry about
a few weeks ago. I needed to believe that,
I didn't say. Because he wouldn't have understood
milk dropping a dozen years late,
a rogue lactation mastitis,
my hope that it would resolve . . . on its own.
"I found my cancer," I said,
before he x-rayed my lungs,
while I removed my bra behind the curtain
(the radiology technician asked me).
How did they find your cancer?

Abecedary of Chemotherapy

after Laura Kolbe

Anticoagulants flow first, clearing the way.
Blood return lets them know veins are ready.
Chemotherapy hopefully kills the cancer.
Digestive cells die, and
epidermal layers, also hair
follicles, although that is later.
Gas builds and you burp,
heartburn flares, worse than the worst
indigestion, like something
jamming your chest,
knocking against the heart,
lungs heavy and tight.
Memory is lost, the mind
numbed by endless nausea.
Oral hygiene might prevent
painful pustules in the mouth that make you
question your food choices.
Remember your last full meal?
Stay home during your nadir, safe from germs,
tiny terrorists of your now fragile
unreactive immune system.
Victim of increasing fatigue, you
watch the world move on, enduring each infusion,
x-ing events out of your calendar, each day
yearning for certainty, for confirmation of shrinkage,
zero-sum game odds, for the win.

Presurgical Scan

I open my e-chart, choose PET scan,
click on "view images" and a row
of stills appears, white ovals and dots
suddenly coming to life as I scroll.
When I press "play," my bones grow and shrink,
organs swell over and over on replay,
a cartoon balloon body inflating, deflating:
skull, heart, liver, empty womb cavity
a white lump, breasts splayed to the sides.
I rotate one ghostly full-length image laterally,
spin my body left and right, until disoriented,
I can't tell if my specter lies face up or down.
I remember praying while the camera spun
over and under me in its donut pathway.
The praying needs to happen earlier,
I think, because the images will only show
what is there, too late for a miracle cure.
I see white smudges "lighting up," as they say,
in my right breast, the cancer taking up
radioactive sugar. The left breast is nearly
translucent, a U-shaped outline, a Roma
tomato swelling out from the vine.
I am ready for the harvest. My prayer:
take what is hungering, leave the rest.

Radiant Hope

The arm of the radiation machine arcs across,
delivering invisible fire that doesn't go out,
an offering in hope, a prayer for cancer to stall.

Each week, my skin reddens. The dutiful techs gloss
over this burn, a necessary omission: no doubts
in the army of radiation. The machine arcs across,

assault aimed at margins and nodes, but I'll need a posse
if the cancer regroups. Meantime, this daily bout
is relentless prayer, hopeful that cancer just gets lost,

goes away. I visualize the goal, try not to boss
my body, but submit to treatment, believing, not proud.
From the arm of the machine, radiation crosses

through tissue to my back. The beams draw
a butterfly shape, a secondary burn loud
and bright as hope, wings of prayer that fall

as skin tightens, then peels. My life remains paused:
no working, no travel, nor out and about.
I endure radiation daily. The machine arcs across,

repetitive as prayer, hope reverent as a canticle.

Radiation Bestiary

Spring arrives early, a hot blaze
to tree eyes smarted by gusty winds.
Brave blooms are colorful tears bruising
underfoot. Skinny limbs trill green;
songbirds sprout leaves. The maple bleeds
abundant wings that will never fly.
I sear and overheat.

My chest absorbs the daily rays,
sheds bark in flakes, eagerly crusts
yellow sap. Insects burrow home.
I endure gores of woodpecker
in staccato, the scrape of hawk talons:
I am raw.

What good can come of so much?

Directions

This is how to survive cancer treatment.
Take a short walk every day, meander
through the neighborhood, wave to the people,
watch birds in flight, in the trees. Whichever
birds you see will do: the grackles hopping
from bush to grass, doves cooing lullabies
in the eaves, songbirds practicing, herons
staring, egrets stalking the shallows, ducks
floating on a pond, cardinals bathing, jays
squawking at the squirrels. When you return, sit
and remember what you saw, write the sounds
in a journal, draw wings. Birds will free you
from nausea, from self-pity, help you
to rest and sleep, to heal and dream, be free.

Found: Letters and Advertisements One Year After Diagnosis

Patient Reminder

Thank you

for choosing At age forty,

screening. discuss

risk,

Records indicate breast

routine health.

mammogram.

If you

Breast

cancer already,

easier disregard.

Early Detection

Breast Care Center
specialists review,
track results.

Time changes,
family history
so important.

Latest technology,
certified,
acceptance,
insurance:
scan to schedule.

You opted in.

You opted in:
scan to schedule
insurance acceptance.

Certified latest technology
so important.

Family history, time,
changes. Track results,
specialists review.

—Breast Care Center

Peace of Mind

| Making | history, | every | breast |
| mammogram. | Prioritize | well-being | today! |

Advanced Screenings

Cutting-edge breast
lumps and abnormalities

available,
most locations.
You were sourced.

To My Chest Muscles, for Defending Against an Implantable Port, One Year Later

I can feel the armor you have built,
or maybe it's a weapon, a stout club
to beat the surgeon's knife,
to resist and smash the next port
instead of bleeding into the hole,
filling the cavity until the box
floats, my chest ballooning into pain.
You lost that battle, blood drained,
artery sewn closed,
port secured and ready
to connect needles with veins.

Still rebelling, you allowed
healing fibers to grow and block
access, you shifted the box,
lower, to the right,
let the flexible base bunch up
at the edge, anything to save me
from chemotherapy,
immunotherapy,
steroids, anti-nausea meds,
from anticoagulants,
antihistamines,
and electrolytes,
especially magnesium,
because who wants
all that dripping slowly

into the heart,
destroying blood and guts,
forcing kidneys into overdrive,
inflaming liver,
for a chance?

Because one year later,
port six months removed,
I find your knot under skin
and wonder: is this a new tumor,
or simply another scar?

II

Locally Recurrent

Hues the Rainbow Reveals

Red colors magnolia seeds
and the Adriamycin pushed
slowly into my veins,
punch-colored blood
carrying poison to every cell.
Orange paints sky and clouds,
peaches' soft skin,
the nausea haunting my gut,
and undersides of eyelids.
Yellow tinges the supermoon,
snowy egrets' feet, fatigue
gnawing, a hazy brain fog.
Green grows the mint,
algae on wet steamy ground,
hair follicles reactivating
on bald skin, the bruise
from last week's blood draw.
Blue stains the sky,
a jay feather, hope
like a pale robin egg,
my now empty tumor site
mushy as blueberry skins.
Indigo wishes to be known,
as I wish my cancer extinct,
a lost history. Violet vibrates
in the heart of figs,

swells the eggplant,
a slow violence
like a tumor that grows,
grows again.

Animal Vegetable Mineral

Mammaries untrue, lymphatics tricked,
antibodies absent: flora's
leaves, traces of soil, metal salts
transformed into treatments, not cures.
Liquid infused, solid consumed,
my cells are festooned, yet cancer lingers.

Oh fragile flesh, oh life
undermined, oh health in decline.
Fauna of sky, beasts of bayou,
you creatures continue, the sea and stars
go on, go on.

Postsurgical Confessions

I may have helped the surgeon's glue
remove itself from my healing chest.
One clump may have covered a clot,
and the wound may have seeped,
fluid slowly sloshing through the long rent,
a pier awash with insistent tides.

Also, there may be stiff wires
curling out like lost fishing line,
and suture thread wiggling free,
a small thin worm baited, unused.

My chest may be a lake surface,
the scar an unwelcome but necessary
long cast seeking sustainability,
a balance of preserve and reap.

I Am the Shores

for Laura Cesarco Eglin

My skin, sand under golden sun,
holes for tiny crabs at rest as the waves
cycle over, my blood pushing both air
and pollutants into pores, seeking
equilibrium: gulls peck the cold eyes
of fish caught in seaweed.

Jagged rocks scar the view as waves
burst into droplets, minute slaps
of pain dulled by repetition. The gulls
cry and hover, search the margins.

Gull's eye view, the shores of my chest
in darkened hues that sharpen on close glide,
a browned flaky coastline am I,
the shallows, marsh seeping to sea.

Stitches

Cancer interrupts your smoothly sewn seam
with too much thread, a knotted mess
that snares your movement, leaves you
wondering how your children will go on.
They do. Their quick moving stitches
leave you behind in a web of thread:
new friends you don't meet, new places
you can't visit, performances you can't attend
because you are stuck in cancer's knot.

You are stalled by chemotherapy,
asleep under the surgeon's knife,
unmoving on the radiation table.
Your children learn independence sewn
in ever widening circles away from you,
away from your tired questions,
the cancer, your attempts
to discuss what it takes from you,
the mother it takes from them.
How can you prepare for the day
your stitches reach the edge,
prepare them for all the sewing after?

In Between Treatments

An afternoon hike without a schedule,
only sunshine, sweet grass, a breeze, shade trees,
insects popping up with a whir when you
walk, a bayou to follow, a rough path
that climbs and drops at will, birds to listen to,
a blue sky, and all of it, all of it,
clearing your mind, even the trash scattered
everywhere, pushed by current, blown by wind,
collected in heaps amidst the flowing
water, guarded by turtles. Ladders they
cannot climb lead only to air, no need
for a clear destination, just a long
slow climb up, like this hike without an end,
an experience, an afternoon, a lull.

Relationship Status: Complicated

Medicine, a stormy lover,
seduces me. I shiver
as chemo caresses my veins.
My bones go hollow, the marrow,
too faint, revives overly blushed.
We meet this way for many months
before my lover removes a tumor
of harsh indecision, yet we proceed
slowly. When I am ready for more,
my skin flames under searing gaze,
every day. I peel away, remade,
no longer passive. I consume
my lover, soak it into every cell.

I become the despised, my love the storm.

The Femme Explains Her Deconstruction

Obviously, the balding head, yet some women
rock it just as well, or better than men. Not so much
a self-centered focus on my own needs and wants,
but removal of a breast for sure changes the contours
of the chest. Then there is hormone suppression,
because who needs hormones advertising your gender?
Well, the burping and the passing gas might confuse
some, especially combined with forgotten dates and names.
I have lost the energy for housework or cooking,
and sleep as much as I dare. I control the TV remote.
My pain, my nausea, my new toilet schedule
are more important than driving the children or errands.
After chest tattoos for radiation, why not tattoo
the surgical scars? I stop noticing the clutter on the counter
because my personal drug store stash must be ready.
One day, I discover new sideburn facial hair
and curse everything because I fucking have cancer.

Self and Other Findings

"Where does the scar end and the self begin?"
—Megan Kim, "My Name Means *PEARL*"

Notice, see, palpate, wait.
Re-palpate, wait. Call, question.
Palpate, compare, schedule—
                    the self ends at carcinoma—

image, compare, re-image. Extract,
slice, re-slice, magnify, compare,
categorize, stain, diagnose
                    a high-grade possession:

receptors, no, immunoreactive, no.
Confirm, report, review, sign,
send. Call, explain, refer—
                    exorcism will create many scars—

medicate, cut, excise, burn.
Extract, slice, magnify, compare.
Re-medicate, recut, remove, reburn
                    the self the damage : the scars the self.

Begin.

III

Metastasized

If you think about it,

we are all dying
slowly, every breath
of air, each cell
dividing, replacing itself.
We are too busy
living to notice,
busy breathing, dividing,
slowly replacing.

Breathing, but as cartilage
fades away, unreplaced,
and joints ache,
still too busy to think
about our dying.
Even so, we breathe,
cells divide and replace,
cholesterol builds
in our arteries,
mucus clogs our lungs.

Busy cells divide,
replace, mutate unchecked
into something new,
ignored until we ache,
until we slow
our living, more aware
of our body now less
slowly dying
than before,

not always replacing,
yet still dividing,
still building,
breathing.

Poem Serum

after Ron Padgett

My cancer markers have risen again,
almost two years
since I found a lump hiding
behind underwire, and I think,
"we have to cancel our trips, delay
the quinceañera." I try to comfort myself
with the idea that I have never heard about
someone dying while planning a quince.

Padgett claims no one dies writing a poem.
I write a poem every day, create
more momentum in verse than hope
for travel, for celebration, as much as birds
moving in flight, their wings the immortal meter
that never stops, merely rises and falls.

Boring and Routine

"My own cancer has become boring and routine"
—Jenny Burkholder, "Water Skiing"

Chemotherapy mists
the memory, hides details
in cottony haze,
while nausea resettles
in the lows of my stomach
like a homesteader,
and I just want my boring
mornings back, my routine:
to walk by the bayou,
watch the birds, listen,
bees hovering on flowers.

My cancer has become
a model of creative survival,
efficient extension,
a routine of return,
relapses into the mundane.
Each appearance nonchalant.
I should expect it, say,
Oh, yes—there you are,
ordinary as breeze,
blasé as the bayou.
I thought you might have gone,
but it was only the fog.
My cancer, my companion,

routine as walking,
basic as birds,
regular as bees.

Seeking

If I were to hike
the bloody trails of my body
like a conservation biologist,
seeking invasive species
to mark, would I see
beyond the scarred holes
of previous uproots?
The empty cave
of my womb is too dry
for anything to grow again,
but the flattened and scorched
clearing of my right breast
is a fresh mar on the landscape.
How can I locate the roots
of cancer that grows
deep under the loamy flesh,
beyond the burn's reach?
Like a fungus
that abides in the soil,
following minute pathways,
leaching into crevices
of least resistance,
undetected,
cancer waits,
cancer watches,
ready to tendril into new
untouched regions
of my body, to integrate
into the landscape

until removing it
will require sacrificing
many native species.

Challenging the Colonizer

My cancer will kill me.
This I have known
for months, a certainty
as knowable as my small bones,
my gift for telling stories
in poems, for keeping
family and pain close.
I do not let things go,
not the stories, the poems,
my family, the painful
quest for perfection,
and now, not this cancer,
relentless as manifest destiny,
its growth a greed
of pioneering, hubris,
blind appropriation.

I know I must keep hope,
let a miracle grow
like the winding heart
of a hurricane, swell
like a rip current's
sweeping vortex, belch
like an earthen tear
spews boulders and lava.
I must become inhospitable
ground, reject cancer's claim
on my body, my life,
must let go instead of keep,

become my own force
of perfect destruction,
wildfire run amok,
tsunami sweeping it all
into the salty sea,
a damaged landscape
unforgiving as drought,
an underworld
to avoid and overlook.

Microcosm

"How is it that we live
mindlessly from one moment to the next?"
—Dorianne Laux, "Breathe"

My world compacts
to house and treatments,
the bayou that I walk,
birds that arrive and depart.

My microscopic cancer
treads with me,
nesting in lymph nodes,
waxing in cycles,
like a tiny new galaxy
with fertile clumps of gas
birthing young bright suns.
They build microsystems,
living mindlessly
within my systems,
in the moment,
so unaware of my small
shortening life
as the boundary
of their minute expansions,
unaware that their growth
will be my end.

But, at my end,
I will shrink
even smaller, contract

into a black hole.
I will unmake
all those little worlds
in the crushing dark,
an everlasting night,
strong within me.

Easy

"as if it was easy for the world to make flowers"
—Ada Limón, "In the Shadow"

Dependable like sunlight, color
bursts onto every berm and field,
seemingly effortless, a new season
appearing overnight, as if flowers
make the world, such making
easy as opening a bloom,
easy as breath, a sigh in the dark.

If only each of us could exhale
flowers, see the beauty we birth
as we breathe, the blossoms
teeming with potential,
with connection, a belonging
easy as color belongs to flowers,
easy as hope, budding in a field.

The Least

I am two days into this round,
with more side effects than usual:
burning legs, painful teeth,
hollow gassy stomach,
nausea that prevents sleep.
Food and water taste like coins
that sit unmoving in my colon.
When I go to the garage to soothe
the car alarm, a large mosquito,
already red with blood,
yet still hungry enough
to drink, finds me.

To save it and me, I slap her flat,
red sloshing onto my skin
bright as a cardinal's crest,
a lizard's full throat.
The abdomen is striped,
now empty of nourishing blood,
and the eggs she would have laid
will never hatch, doomed
by my slap, or by DNA breaks
from their mother's last drink.

But, how can I know
what our ravaged earth
requires from mosquitos?
They lay eggs amid rusty cans
that wait for acidic rain to ripen

into larvae that swim
around plastic wrappers, breathe
air laden with pollution fumes.
Chemotherapy laced blood
may be the least of this mosquito's
mother worries in her short life,
just a meal, like chemotherapy
is a means, a method
not of nourish, but extinguish,
because with my own growing
symptoms, with more infusions
to absorb, how can I know
what she and they and I,
what any of us,
will endure to survive?

Without End

after ire'ne lara silva

I want to be infinite,
to transform within,
become other
as cancer mutates.

I want to be forever
an unforgiving storm
with infinite lightning,
eternal precision strikes
scorching new cancer cells.
My reverberating thunder
will absorb rising sounds
boiling from the burns
as my storm clouds
grow with the vapors,
leave the strike zones dry
as a long-receded shore.
The scar tissue will crystallize,
become salt that will sting
the last raw remnant,
any small strand or sequence,
salt that will seep
into every sliver, destroy
all cancerous impulses.

My body will be
an infinite vigilance
protecting my original,

unmutated cells,
the endless immunity
we all assume
is diligently working,
deep and loyal
inside our finite selves.
I will be without.

Notes and Acknowledgments

"Abecedary of Chemotherapy" is for Sara Greenslit.

"Easy" is for Erika Solberg.

Thanks to Maria Miranda Maloney for pushing me to give the form of "Found: Letters and Advertisements" more movement, especially in part one and thanks also to Erika Solberg for telling me to expand the title to include "One Year Later."

My gratitude to Laura Cesarco Eglin and Maria Miranda Maloney for workshopping a number of these poems in our monthly meetings, and for giving me the title for "Relationship Status: Complicated."

For sensitivity reading the content, and especially the original title of "The Femme Explains Her Deconstruction," I thank Lee Anne Wilde and her children. Lee Anne also helped me work through several alternative titles before we found the one that worked best.

For being my first readers, and for providing feedback on individual poems and my musings about this collection, my gratitude to Sara Greenslit and Erika Solberg.

I appreciate the specific encouragement and support for all of my writing, and especially these poems, from James Sheridan, Jennifer Bown, and Elena Radulescu.

I wish to thank the editors of the following journals and anthologies where these poems have been published or are forthcoming, some in slightly different versions.

American Journal of Nursing: "Presurgical Scan"

Amethyst Review: "Easy"

Ars Medica: "Abecedary of Chemotherapy," "Found: Patient Reminder," and "To My Chest Muscles, for Defending Against an Implantable Port, One Year Later"

The Bayou Review: "The Body Betrays"

equinox: "I Am the Shores"

Habits: the Good, the Bad, and the Ugly, Public Poetry Press: "Directions"

Huizache: "Challenging the Colonizer" and "The Femme Explains Her Deconstruction"

Last Stanza Poetry Journal: "Boring and Routine"

Light Shines, then Leaves on Spreading Trees: The Friendswood Poets Anthology, Friends of the Friendswood Public Library: "Abecedary of Chemotherapy," "Hues the Rainbow Reveals," "In Between Treatments," and "Poem Serum"

Rogue Agent: "Radiant Hope" and "Seeking"

The Senior Class: 100 Poems on Aging, Lamar University Literary Press: "Microcosm"

Sky, Land, Water: Womxn Weaving Nature, Mouthfeel Press: "The Least" and "Poem Serum"

Southern Humanities Review: "Radiation Bestiary"

Sunflowers Rising: Peace Poems, Sunflower Poetry Society of Kansas: "Easy"

Texas Poetry Assignment: "Stitches"

About the Author

Elisa A. Garza is a poet, editor, and writing teacher. Her full-length collection *Regalos* (Lamar University Literary Press) was a finalist for the National Poetry Series and one of its poems was exhibited at The Health Museum in Houston. Elisa's chapbook *Between the Light / entre la claridad* (Mouthfeel Press) is in a second edition. She teaches writing workshops for cancer patients and survivors. Connect with her on the Poetry by Elisa A. Garza Facebook page.